Book of the
Beginning

M.J. Sung

WestBow Press books may be ordered through booksellers or by contacting:

WestBow Press
A Division of Thomas Nelson & Zondervan
1663 Liberty Drive
Bloomington, IN 47403
www.westbowpress.com
844-714-3454

Interior Image Credit: Jingjing

- Scripture quotations marked ESV taken from The Holy Bible, English Standard Version® (ESV®), Copyright © 2001 by Crossway, a publishing ministry of Good News Publishers. All rights reserved.
- Scripture quotations marked NLT are taken from the Holy Bible, New Living Translation, Copyright © 1996, 2004, 2015 by Tyndale House Foundation. Used by permission of Tyndale House Publishers, Inc., Carol Stream, Illinois 60188. All rights reserved.
- Scripture quotations marked NASB are taken from The New American Standard Bible®, Copyright © 1960, 1962, 1963, 1968, 1971, 1972, 1973, 1975, 1977, 1995 by The Lockman Foundation. Used by permission.
- Scripture quotations marked NIV are taken from The Holy Bible, New International Version®, NIV® Copyright © 1973, 1978, 1984, 2011 by Biblica, Inc.® Used by permission. All rights reserved worldwide.
- Scripture quotations marked NKJV are taken from the New King James Version®. Copyright © 1982 by Thomas Nelson. Used by permission. All rights reserved.
- Scripture quotations marked AKJV are taken from the Authorized King James Version.
- Scripture quotations marked ASV are taken from the Holy Bible, American Standard Version (The Revised Version, American Standard Edition of the Bible). Public domain.
- Scripture quotations marked CEV are taken from the Contemporary English Version®, Copyright © 1995 American Bible Society. All rights reserved.

ISBN: 978-1-9736-9039-9 (sc)
ISBN: 978-1-9736-9040-5 (e)

Library of Congress Control Number: 2020907000

Print information available on the last page.

WestBow Press rev. date: 10/15/2020

WESTBOW
PRESS®
A DIVISION OF THOMAS NELSON
& ZONDERVAN

Book of the
Beginning

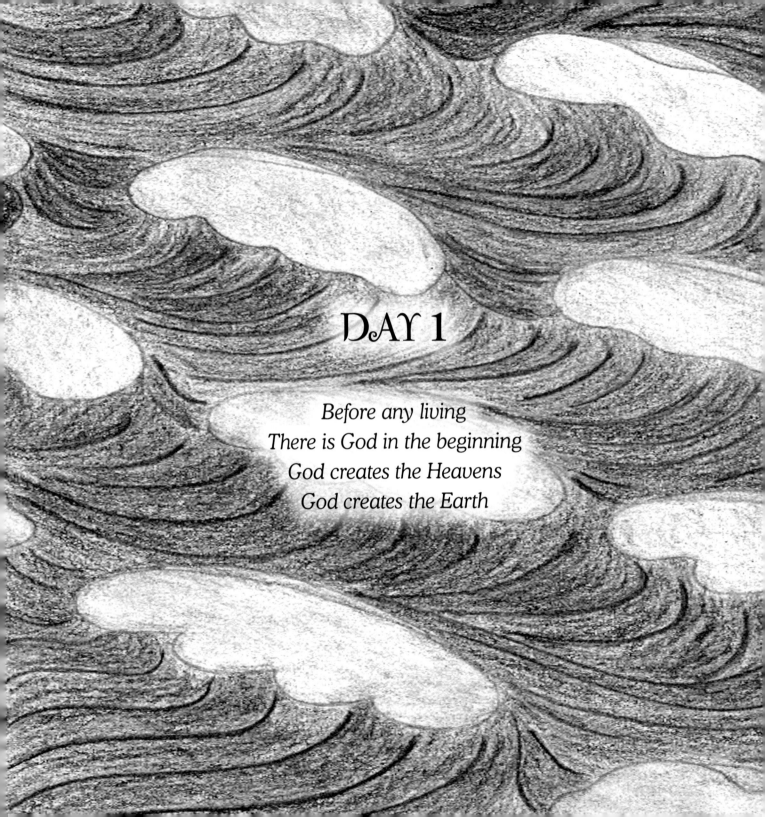

DAY 1

Before any living
There is God in the beginning
God creates the Heavens
God creates the Earth

The Earth is born
But the Earth has no form
Over the deep
With darkness covered
Over the waters
The Spirit of God hovers

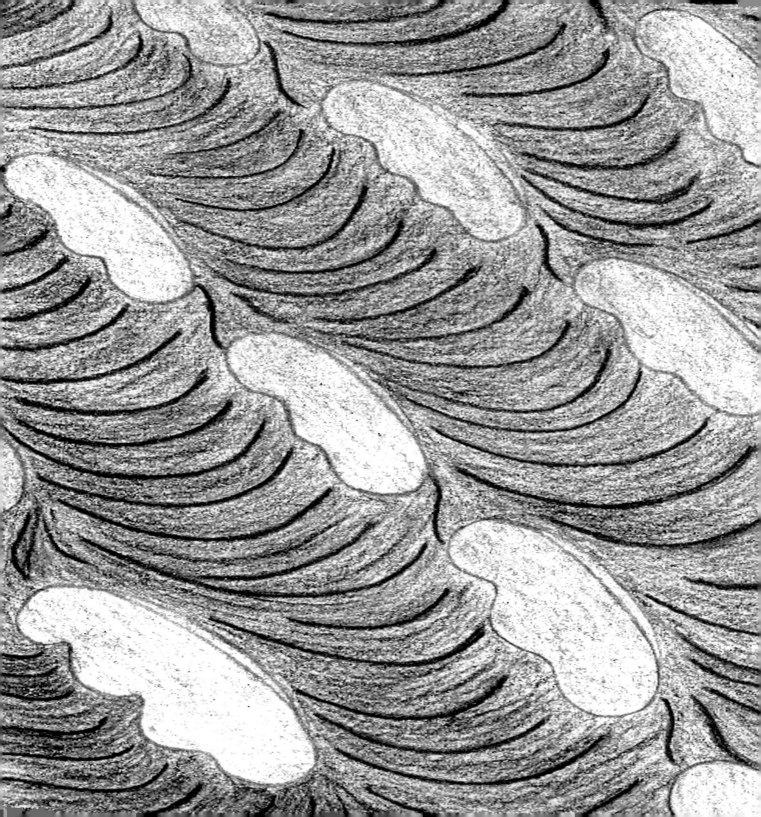

"Let there be light" *(ESV Gen 1:3)*
Did God say
Then there is light
And God calls the light "Day" *(ESV Gen 1:5)*

God sees that the light
Is good in his sight
So God separates the light
From the darkness he calls "Night" *(ESV Gen 1:5)*

There was evening
There was morning
The first day of the story

DAY 2

On this day God proclaims
"Let there be a space" *(NLT Gen 1:6)*
"And let it separate" *(NASB Gen 1:6)*
"The waters from the waters" *(NASB Gen 1:6)*

The waters make way
From above and below
God says it and it is so

God calls the space "Heaven" (ESV Gen 1:8)
Since then it has stayed
Evening left
Morning came
Blessed was the second day

DAY 3

Then God says here
"Let the waters beneath the sky" (NLT Gen 1:9)
"Flow together into one place" (NLT Gen 1:9)
"So dry ground may appear" (NLT Gen 1:9)

God calls the dry ground "Land" (NIV Gen 1:10)
God calls the waters "Seas" (NIV Gen 1:10)
God sees that it is good
And good it is indeed

Then God says with creation
"Let the land sprout with vegetation" (NLT Gen 1:11)
"Plants yielding seeds!" (ESV Gen 1:11)
"And fruit trees bearing fruit" (ESV Gen 1:11)
"In which is their seed" (ESV Gen 1:11)

Their seeds will then make
Fruits of the same
What God says happens
And is what arranged

God also sees this as good

There was evening
There was morning
The third day was set put

DAY 4

Then God says this time
"Let there be lights" (NIV Gen 1:14)
"In the vault of the sky" (NIV Gen 1:14)
"To separate the Day from the Night" (NIV Gen 1:14)

"And let them serve as signs to mark sacred times" (NIV Gen 1:14)

"Let these lights in the sky" (NIV Gen 1:15)

"Shine down on the earth" (NIV Gen 1:15)

As it is told

It is so

God makes two great lights
The greater ruling Day
The lesser ruling Night
God also makes stars
Scattering far and wide

God sets this in place
In the midst of space
And God sees that it is good

Evening passed
Morning came
Worthy was the fourth day

DAY 5

Then God says with might
"Let the skies be filled" (NLT Gen 1:20)
"With birds of every kind!" (NLT Gen 1:20)

"Let the waters swarm" (NLT Gen 1:20)
"With fish and other life!" (NLT Gen 1:20)

So God creates great creatures
Of the skies and of the seas

Every living and moving thing
With which the water teems
God sees it is good
And God blesses them because he could

So God says to the creatures
"Be fruitful and multiply!" (NLT Gen 1:22)

"Fill the waters in the seas" (ESV Gen 1:22)
"And let the birds increase on the earth" (NIV Gen 1:22)

There was evening
There was morning
The fifth day achieved

DAY 6

Then God says with force
"Let the earth bring forth" *(ESV Gen 1:24)*
"Every sort of animal" *(NLT Gen 1:24)*

"Livestock and creeping things" *(ESV Gen 1:24)*

"Large and small" *(Good News Translation Gen 1:24)*

"Each according to its kind" *(NKJV Gen 1:24)*

The word becomes tangible
God makes all sorts of wild animals

The weak and the proud
Livestock and small animals
That creep the ground

Each to its kind
producing its offspring

It is as they should
And God sees that it's good

Then God says with excitement
"*Let us make mankind in our image*" (NIV Gen 1:26)
"*In our likeness!*" (NIV Gen 1:26)
"*They will reign over the fish in the sea!*" (NLT Gen 1:26)

"*The birds of the sky*" (NLT Gen 1:26)
"*The livestock*" (NLT Gen 1:26)

"*Over all the earth and over every creeping thing*" (ESV Gen 1:26)

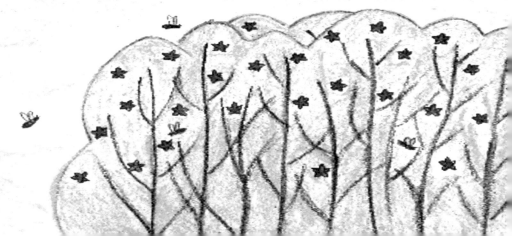

So God creates man in his own image
In the image of God he creates him
Male and female he creates them

Then God blesses them saying with life
"Be fruitful and multiply" (NLT Gen 1:28)
"Fill the earth and subdue it!"(ESV Gen 1:28)
"Rule over the fish in the sea"(NIV Gen 1:28)
"The birds of the sky" (NIV Gen 1:28)
"And over every living thing that moves!" (ESV Gen 1:28)

Then God says with truth
"Look! I have given you!" (NLT Gen 1:29)
"Every plant yielding seed" (ESV Gen 1:29)
"And every tree with seed in its fruit" (ESV Gen 1:29)
"On the face of all the earth" (AKJV Gen 1:29)
"To you it shall be for food" (ASV Gen 1:29)
"And to every beast" (ESV Gen 1:30)
"And to every bird" (ESV Gen 1:30)

"To everything that creeps on the earth" (ESV Gen 1:30)
"For everything else that breathes" (CEV Gen 1:30)
"I give every green plant for food!" (NIV Gen 1:30)

And it is so
God sees all that he'd made
And behold it is very good
Evening passed
Morning came
God's glorious sixth day

DAY 7

*Thus the heavens and earth are completed
In all their vast array
All of God's work has meaning
It's the dawn of his grand display*

So God blesses the seventh day
Holy is it made
God rests from his work of creation

Like the poetry and harmony of this book, the
world would not go 'round without the support
of all the salt and light people like you.

Half of all proceeds from this book will be
donated to Operation Dawn Gospel Rehab
A non-profit organization that provides rehabilitation
services all around the world and are dedicated to supporting
long term recovery through faith for those in need
If you would like to learn more about
this charitable organization
Please visit www.OPDawn.org

ABOUT THE AUTHOR

Marvin "M.J." Sung was born and raised in New York City. Though he grew up outside the faith community, God captured his heart in 2013. Marvin believes everyone should have the opportunity to hear about the bible, especially at a young age. His inspiration comes from meditating on God's word. Marvin hopes this book will plant a seed of light in the children of this generation and the next to come.

Printed in the United States
By Bookmasters